I0201442

*

𝔇𝔬𝔰𝔢

Poems of Quintessential Ethereality

Brad Dehler

TROIKA PUBLISHNG
SALEM, OREGON

*

Dose: Poems of Quintessential Ethereality

Copyright © Brad Dehler 2016

ALL RIGHTS RESERVED. No part of this work covered by the
copyright herein may be reproduced, transmitted, stored, or used in any
form or by any means graphic, electronic, or mechanical, including but
not limited to photocopying, recording, scanning, digitizing, taping, Web
distribution, information networks, or information storage and retrieval
systems, except as permitted under Section 107 or 108 of the 1976 United
States Copyright Act, without the prior written permission of the author.

Printed in the United States of America
First edition

Additional copies are available at
https://www.createspace.com/3514742
or www.Amazon.com

For product information, permission to use material
from this text, or further permissions questions- please
e-mail to: Troika7@gmail.com

Book design and layout: Brad Dehler
Both photographs: painting by and portrait of the author

ISBN-13: 978-0-9829733-1-8
ISBN-10: 0-982-97331-4

Troika Publishing; Salem, Oregon
Printing by CreateSpace; Charlotte, South Carolina
An Amazon Company
USA

Other Troika Publishing books by Brad Dehler:
Cantus: A Book of Poems
(ISBN-13: 978-0-982-97330-1 & ISBN-10: 0-982-97330-6)
https://www.createspace.com/3481170
http://www.amazon.com/Cantus-Brad-Dehler/dp/0982973306/

*

"(The) rhyme and images and musings... are intriguing. (Brad is) a deep thinker, thought provoking... on a quest to find meaning and treasures in life"

-**Millie Renfrow** Seattle Poetess; Co-author of "Between Light and Shade", recipient of the Phyllis Ennes award, and Associate of Seattle's "It's About Time Writing Series"

*

4

*

DOSE
Table of Contents

*

*

*

*

*

INTRODUCTION
DOSE

Thank you for choosing Dose. This is my sophomore book, succeeding my first book "Cantus". I chose the title "Dose" for various reasons. First off, I want to minimize the preconceptions that follow labeling, minimal in one word. Another reason is that I hope that these words, stanzas, poems are healing and supportive of life- as a dose of true medicine. Finally, the title phonetically resembles the word "dos" which means "two" in Spanish.

Why Cantus? Why can't we? Why Dose? Why don't we? Where Cantus was me, stepping out in "singing", my vocation out loud; Dose is a second offering that again collects poems from the past and present -to be read in the future with a focus on internal change. We are in this life together for the time being. The questions and conclusions posited here are a call to action for which all are accountable. These imperatives absolutely include me. I have not perfected what I propose within the text, I attempt to display it as it is revealed to me.

These poems are medicine as well as a challenge. It can be bitter and unpleasant, confounding and triumphant. The only way it works, though, is by internalizing. I hope that you find these poems relevant to your life- and with that, integrated in a universal human experience.

*

I composed these poems in various States and
various phases of my life. I began writing at age
thirteen and instantly knew that there was a
message to record and that the message was greater
than I am. Take each poem slowly, removed from the
regular toil of daily life. Enter a reflective and
meditative state. Then perhaps what I offer here
can take it further.

The title of each poem is based on a specific line
of that particular poem. I do this to reduce
convoluting the message.

The formula is organic; I attempt to remove over
thinking and meddling with words- to avoid
superseding the message, to place the words close
to how they arrive initially in mind. I have
learned to reduce contrived manipulation. This is
where I believe the heart and head converge fairly
equitably.

Now step out, lay back and remove yourself from the
day-to-day. Take the Dose.

*

Do not tremble in the dark
For that which lurks
    In the dark
Trembles in the light
Bring forth the light

New Orleans 07.06.05

*

Golden heart be attentive
Rubber souls get walked on
A faultless vase
    Resonates with a knock
The audience
    Does not have it all
    On the line
So decision should be made
    From within

                    Salem 01.09.11

*

All the blended fruits
    Of the merriment
All the twisted troops
    Of the regiment
All the moments that
    Make the momentum
What is the path?
    A mazy glade?
    A suspended balance beam?
Something in your efforts
    And once passed up
It is missing
    It is missed
Set out on
    The Hallowed venture
To end remiss

                          Salem 03.23.08

*

Something so magnificent
   By its presence
   Bends your knee
Loss of dominance
   In your element

                    Corvallis 2000

*

Future is illusion
Past is delusion
All we have is
    Now

                              Salem 08.31.10

*

Broken hopes on slippery slopes
Hope into the void
    When devoid of hope
Ridiculous to believe in it
    While in acquisition
Though destined are the
    Fruits of fruition
The struggle can produce
    Self-fulfilled prophesy
Awareness is fundamental
We are poor prophets
    And sightless psychics
Hopeless in our misfortunes
Kindle that peat moss
    For future torch

Portland 10.18.15

*

Bless me
So that I can bless you
Bless you
So that you can bless others
We are all now keen
Our lives richer

                    Salem 03.17.13

*

There is a troika
    Heading in a direction
In attempts to salvage
The perishable
We are apathetic or preoccupied
We are not responsible
Until
What is in us is entropic
    Or sinister occupation
The third horse, most powerful
    Able for change in direction
    Is the choice
The glorious change is
    Salvation of permanence

                        Salem 2007

*

When time is right
There is nothing sweeter
Than salty sweat

Salem 10.23.13

*

You are occupied territory
Not to be preoccupied
    With recognition
Aim to remain re-occupied
Possessed by the spirit

Modoc Forest, CA 06.23.16

*

Take a trip
Everywhere I go,
    I take my life there
Those actions ascribed
    To those every moments
Take a hiatus
    Anywhere
Right here
Had a sensation though
Could not determine which
    Sense told me so
Take out of here
Give it to what
    Was stifled inside

Salem 08.09.10

*

Introspective
Make for change
Night time revival

Utah 1998

*

A child looks up to adults
As a great mystery
    Full of understanding
The assumption is that age
Takes the climb up the mountain
The truth is that most
    Wallow down at basecamp

New Orleans 2005

*

```
The things I imagined
Are really not as great
But those things in the expanse
Far exceeding my imagination
```

Salem 2009

*

Beware inertia
Bodies at rest
Motion against resistance
    Imbibing to gravity
Anger perpetuates
The waves surge into us
    I am charged
Stand up, gear up
    I leave armed

                Salem 04.21.11

*

There is a chorus from
    The meadows
Time has come to stop and
    Inhale deep
Steam rising from your brow
Stopped to make camp
    That was then
    The tremor time
A prost to your good work
    This far, thus far

See now
    New and lavish arising
The Kinnikinnick travels with
Goodbye familiar friend
    Hello new curious friend
The winds started as a whisper
    Something light
Just enough to lift a feather
The wind escalating
Send some Kinnikinnick down
The earth is quaking underfoot
In the advent of immanence
    Imminently in the air
Revelatory nature
This woman
    Walks alone in the crowd
    She makes sound
    Within the noise

                    Albany, OR 06.2011

                    27

*

Do you understand
That I am just a man
My actions can be superhuman
    Reach past my will
My ideas are super-hue
... Would lead to love eventually
The mythic beast of
    Desire quenched
Came alive

                    Salem 04.18.11

*

I thought it impossible
    To satiate this voracious
    Appetite
Have these passing years
    Lulled the dragon to sleep?
I was once like a goldfish
    With propensity to binge
    All the way to death
Believing that the latest bite
    May be the last
Bite as hindsight
    Revealed the mere filler

Our love contains nutrients
    Truly resolving hunger
Alas I hunger again,
Alas I'll always love you again

                    Salem 04.30.08

*

Do not worry
I have a gun
They declared martial law
Times like these
    Taking to head counting
Others taking headshots
The sum
    Is not the person

                    New Orleans 07.20.06

*

Attaché attached to desolation
The wounded still-twitch
Baggage sighted oblivion
All in need
Do not tend to your deficiencies
This world is poor
    When we cannot put
    Our deficiencies aside
Curves seduce
The paved way slides from underfoot

Salem 12.08.10

*

I was prepared to evacuate my house
I was not ready to evacuate my city
It was a season of migration
New refugee
Legends without recorded histories
A walk amongst kings
    Few and far between
Closest thing to divinity
    Engendered in nature
It was the forest
    That invited the silence
And it was the silence
    That invited the quiet

                    Flower Mound, TX 10.2005

*

Feel not threatened
    By the questions
The questions exist
    Without their posing

                    Salem 02.11.11

*

For the exhaulted,
There must be one
    Taking number
    Away from the glory

                    Salem 11.18.10

*

Enigmatizing
What is plain in front of you
Serving the purpose
    Of serving yourself
Abandoning the duty
    Of bridging the gap
Between right and wrong
So
When the contrary
Is evidenced forth
You have sided
As enemy of truth

                    Portland, OR 01.22.10

*

Unconscious hours
Are swept, slept through
There are frontiers yet still
Doubt tells you it's been covered
But new eyes
     Open new worlds

                    Salem 06.03.11

*

Future is illusion
    Past is delusion
All we have is now

            Salem 08.31.10

*

Clouds do not float
    They are falling
I grew and stumbled
    Upon rocks
I was challenged
    By great fields
And intimidated by the forest
Water; lifesource
I was summoned
    As we all are
To the ocean
It is and I loved
The tide rolled and
I float vulnerable

                    Salem 04.17.06

*

Those in avid belief
    That lessons are only learned
    Through experience
Close their ears to sirens
For a second's satisfaction

                Corvallis, OR 05.09.1999

*

You asked our age
    And assumed limits
We told you
But we did not ask of yours

That would be rude

You asked to share land
We opened our arms
    Knowing it is a part
    Of all of us
You poisoned yourself
    Burned, scorched, and sold
Our land in jeopardy

                    Portland, OR 02.14.11

*

Always thinking throughways
Could not predict sunken sideways
All those messages
    That do not have voices
All those worthy voices
    I did not receive
Come back down
    I see now folly

                    Salem 06.04.11

*

Anatomy of a car crash
When distracted
Attention switches to
    Arising situation
The argument
The spilled water
Most urgent because most emergent
Eyes abandon the road
Last assessment of road
    Copacetic

                        Salem 10.23.13

*

It is not
Always head versus heart
What about
    Life through liver

                    Salem 03.25.13

*

No external remedy to distraught
Like a happy pill
    For depression
Energy will not cure
    My exhaustion

New Orleans 07.06.05

*

River of deceit
Dam it
Get lake of fire

Salem 03.20.14

*

There was a troubling sound
That resounded like a voice
Something that gave voice
    To despair
Rousing me from slumber
Seeking signs in imagined shadows
Do another parameter check
No founded proof
Resorting to prayer
In hopes to reach outside my power
Undoubtedly, the demon
    Peered in the open window
And in many hapless acts
    Discovered me, asleep

Salem 07.04.11

*

Administering the shock
    Because we were told so
We accept
We have witnessed
That is how
    We are apathetic
To all this pain

Portland, OR 10.25.15

*

Once you reach your dreams
Won't you come back down?
May the joy of contentment
Be yours

                                    Salem 08.22.11

*

Songs of freedom
Cries of peace
Arriving in concert
To listen to what you
    Want to hear
Misplaced bemoanings
Dad abandoned
    And
Mom did not know how to love
They were lost at sea
    Overwhelmed
You are lost at sea
    Inundated
Drowning
Howling

                    Salem 10.12.15

*

I turn the chapters
Cross the bridges
Nay, I do not burn them

New Orleans 07.09.05

*

Privileged misfits fall
    Within their tier
There is a cheap and fast
satisfaction
    With candy and with anger
A whole other satisfaction
    With bread and butter
Laborers are left behind
After project culmination
Fatigue on the face
    Can look like wisdom
    The apparent knowing smile
Decoding labyrinths
    Glory only within that architect

                Salem 08.30.11

*

```
Inside your contentment
    Are
Latent entities
Known only through serenity
Disturbed,
    They will coup
```

Portland, OR 11.22.10

*

Red heron had been plucked
Feather by feather
No capabilities of flight
Pale placid skin exposed
Yet can be given flight
    By mere man's conjecture

            Salem 03.04.13

*

Ask Yankton
Ask Nakota
Knock lights out
Call it supernova
Tell the new guard
We have been here before
     All along
The vegetation and waterways
     That divide
Yield those who swim and step
Ask those who have trekked
     Climbed, crawled
Good counsel

                              Salem 11.18.10

54

*

Divinity speaks to our souls
We deviate from ourselves
    To not hear our souls
That feeling that won't leave
Of the fall, loss of all

                Corvallis, OR 09.18.01

*

This impending room
Fill it with sights and sounds
My incredulous eyes widen
    As they did
When I scant see nothing at all
Content is not satisfied

                        Salem 08.09.10

*

Do not focus
Too much on the small screens
In the big picture

Corvallis, OR 10.12.1998

*

Retreat from obligation
Surf-ride tides
Disheveled appearance acceptable
I would call it
My days in the sun

Salem 09.01.11

*

That radiating core
Native roots
    Tangled together
    In my carriage
I write in exile
I sing of release

                        Salem 08.31.10

*

An aim that revealed the target
But missed
Such is the world
Without the understanding
Without arrows

                    Portland, OR 01.03.11

*

I felt so alive
I had consumed enough
Not truly fulfilled unless
I had truly hungered

Salem 06.22.11

*

Negotiating,
    Balancing dissatisfaction
Failing beget wagering over waging
Landslide begins
The collapsing landscape
    Clings to its dead
This is a recovery
    Not a rescue

                        Salem 03.28.14

*

When you are
Because you have been
Blessed alumni

Portland, OR 01.16.11

*

When you are that hungry
You have two options
Eat or go to work

                    Salem 07.10.11

*

As you regret shattered glass vase
Left to pick up the shards
What your hands do not grab
Guided by your eyes
Your feet will find

Salem 08.28.10

*

You hapless morose
You desperate lament
You simple sought accomplice
Internal politics leading
    To external threat
Nature to look
    For angel in black
Discover surplus
    Demons in white

                    Salem 07.08.13

*

For years
Earning the way up the floors
One day called to the top
To descend the stairs
Dismissed

Portland, OR 01.15.11

*

Knocking against my will
Open the door
To this glorious mourn
The sun shines on turmoil
Must not let it set
    On regret

Salem 07.22.10

*

Must we be broken
    Before fixing
Our alms out?

                Salem 09.04.10

*

Passion finances the war
    Between the beloved
Conversion to hurt until bankrupt
Will needed to re-collect affinity

                    Portland, OR 11.15.10

*

The pain is a venue
The struggle an avenue
Accessible among the trees
    Within you
I see myself reflected
    In your eyes
Struggles led you to a state
    That was beneath you
Out from your core
It was under your feet
    All along
Keep you grounded
Now you kneel, now you sit
    Now you lay
Dulcet dreams

                    Salem 11.17.10

*

Regardless of any surveys
All I can account for
    Is that those
Who truly know me
Truly love me

                    Portland, OR 11.15.10

*

One can only know others
Once
One knows one's self

                                        Salem 11.18.10

*

The spiritual, philosophical, political
Micro-mezzo-macro
In no particular order
The void pathologizes spirituality
Awareness gives literacy
Gives authority
The oblivious to incompetent
In a moment of zen
    I put it down to pen
To touch paper then beyond

                    Portland, OR 11.29.10

*

```
There is no time
    Except now
So now
    Is the time
```

                                    Salem 11.07.15

*

There is talk about the
    Revolution
Problem
    Rebels have no constitution

                    Portland, OR 11.29.10

*

Oppose our tendencies
Bitterness abounds, inevitable
    Treat with cream & sugar
Bill this world as a debt and credit
    Debt to justice
    Credit to love
To break tendencies
    It takes tending

                    Vancouver, WA 01.2.11

*

I was privileged enough
To cover my eyes
    During the war
Right or wrong
I supported the faction
That would not enslave me

                    Pacific City, OR 07.05.11

*

I want a shot at the title
What to do when I get there?
Exhausted, depleted of resource
Yet the battle is not settled
The privileged are dependent
    Upon the hungry

                            Salem 10.28.10

*

I cannot tell you
    Why to believe in your dreams
Mine have yet to come true
But belief is the only way
    They will
Will they?
Will you?

                    Portland, OR 11.15.10

*

In a state of NOLA
What's more than
    A club in a car
Hatchet in the attic

            New Orleans 08.26.04

*

The trial should be in the mind
But you determined you knew me
    Prior, as a prejudice
So that the jury
    Was out of the sound
And the judge from out of the sight

                    Salem 03.05.14

*

It is a good thing
For the most part
Uh oh
Stop me
Before I start

Corvallis, OR 11.15.1999

*

Any sacrifice is sacred
It is how we
Physically pray

Portland, OR 07.10.11

*

What they will not admit
    Is they never thought much of you
Working your way up
All they want
    Is to take you down

                    Portland, OR 01.20.13

*

The new food is different
An experience
    More acquainted in youth
A curiosity that kept me searching
New and different
Much like love

                    Salem 07.31.11

*

Being aware of what
    They want you to think
Is the first line of defense
Against manipulation
Being aware of how
    They really feel
Is the first steps into insight
Yet beyond all this
    The deep look inside

                    Salem 10.31.13

*

You see those little birds
Harassing a hawk
After a distance
    Most peel away
Yet there is one little bird
    Snipping
The substantially larger hawk abides
Despite all ability
    To conquer the small challenge

                Cloverdale, OR 06.23.13

*

It was only after
    I awoke
That I realized
    I had fallen asleep
And then onset shame
Relent, repent
I have weathered
    Many such storms
This one is different
This one tethered

                    Salem 02.10.13

*

Hanging on every word
    Of an idol
Over issues
    Esoteric, intangible
Inconsequential insignificance
Idle
To my mind, my involved sage
Is to not complicate

                    Portland, OR 02.23.14

*

Let me be a critic
    To the archetype
    As best of friends are
Neither opposer nor supporter
Impossible to separate
    Any persons
    From their paradigm
A thousand rifles
    Far too much
    For one man to handle
Yet
    Far too little
    To defend a nation
Yeah
    The man can recruit
    And nation convert
But consider the bullet that
    Ends the empire's emperor
Incendiary bulleted texts
    With similar aim
    I may offer
For war is too loud
    To hear this offering
And peace time
    May be cannabis to the masses

                    Salem 07.2009

*

Asking why did it mean so much
Stubborn deadlock
Time expired to anguish
Squandered so much
    Did it mean
Why

                        Corvallis, OR 09.30.1998

*

Little did I know
That the vitae
    I submitted
Was part of the dossier
    To destroy me

        Salem 02.01.14

*

Ill niche
Nihilism well played
Worshipped self
You are gone
Your god is dead

                    Portland, OR 02.07.08

*

Dreams are ideas
    Not of this world
For those not handed fortune
Only come to fruition
    With Drive made real
Be ridden of things that do not
    Drive you
Driven by the knowledge of
    All things that could rid you

                    Salem 01.03.11

*

Adopt a highway
Raise it as my own
Only one bathed in sun
Well-traveled
Attach my name
Complexities rising
Take it easy
Meet Keno in Reno

Reno, NV 06.24.16

*

You know more without you
Than within you
More of the moon
Than your ocean
The objective point of view
    Far more piercing

                          Salem 11.29.10

*

Being in untruth
    Your answers are questioned
Getting technical definitions
    Of depravity
    And corruption
Not a failure
    You failed again
Label akin to impossibility
No cycles, new day
Work from memory
    There's the lesson
Recognize
    Pattern the elements
    That cause virtue
Never "not yourself"
    Troubled times- new challenges
Open yourself to greatness
All bridges most valuable
    When the big ones burn

                    Corvallis, OR 2000

*

There is no reality
   Outside my own
   That of which I know
I know paradigm
Equating to two cents

        Salem 11.29.10

*

Your fictional mind
    In a non-fictional world
Quite the imagination
Dim witty
Dragon your fate around
Have mercy on your soul
That plays for keeps
Keeper for reals
I think I will stay
    I like the vibe tonight

Salem 01.08.16

*

This is no cycle for me
It is a one way track
Low hope to come back
Heading toward the storm
Losing my warmth
Reason why we do this
    Coming home
Operating in self
Serving shadows
Relying upon some dark horse

              Portland, OR 10.07.10

*

Living the dream
Feeling life is unreal
Sensing it is surreal
I found myself
      In a situation
And in that situation
      I found myself

                    Salem 12.30.15

*

```
The way it is
     Delivered
Can bring
     Perspective
```

                    Salem 02.18.16

*

Beacon of hope
Bastian of love
Purveyor of charity
The sword and salve of justice
Let me be that for you

Salem 02.01.16

*

Evilness lives on silenced lips
Even a lie invites
    Dialog roots out truth
Power structure resists
    Change and evaluation
There is a continuum
    And it is finite
Theory is ideal
Until put to pavement
A king's portion
    A Cesarean section
The light on in the city
    Turns off the starlight

                    Salem 01.20.11

*

When it comes to pass
The lies
    Will lie down to truth
The confused
    Will kneel and bow and know
The insolent
    Will bow and break
You tamper with lies in illusion
    Of breaking paradigm
I reassure all who
    Have ear to listen
The urgency is to calibrate
    With the know

                              Portland, OR 07.24.09

*

We are both
On this side of hell
And
This side of heaven

              Salem 03.21.15

*

Neither above moral
Nor above morale

                    Corvallis, OR 04.27.1999

*

Rumbling, rolling over the
Great Plains
Opposite the insignificant
No surprise
    The spoils were squandered
Ustoll the soil
Because our hopes are hung
On heroes and stars
Does not mean our hope
    Is suspended

                    Salem 01.22.11

*

Atrocious notions
   When we were kids
Are enacted in our adulthood
   As if licensed by age

                    Salem 01.09.11

*

The Scars that split
    Us in half
Before and after the event
Confusion
    Rendering us duplicitous

                Salem 03.20.16

*

There was a ghost
You breathed your warmth
Into the frozen
    Northern sky
Came back a cold front
Unrecognizable

                    Portland, OR 01.03.11

*

You develop venom
Fangs to inflict
Yours is a kiss
    Of a serpent

            Salem 04.12.16

*

Do not be scared of open places
Everything is in its place
Settle down,
    Just have a seat
Break some bread
    It's more than 'eat'

                    Salem 04.28.16

*

Something grips the heart
Kickstart
In hot pursuit
Corners rounding
Pounding into rhythm
Into an anthem
I got something
I want you to have

Portland, OR 01.03.11

*

For the exalted
There must be one taking number
Away from the glory

                    Salem 11.18.10

*

Not lonely, but lone
Just as I am untrusting, but loan
Now I have been broken down

Corvallis, OR 09.29.1999

*

Living on a dead end
Enter a river bend
Passing time
Skipping river stones
Educated in academia
    When paying intuition

            Vancouver, WA 12.24.10

*

Can you big enough to deliver?
Can you be small enough to care?

Salem 05.18.14

*

We go backwards
But we also go forwards
All the while
Getting closer
We did it together
Making our love

Salem 05.03.16

*

Disregard waging war
    Or peace
Wage preservation
    Of universal value

        Portland, OR 07.24.09

*

I plucked the apple
    From the tree
    For you
I wrote the book
    On your skin
All those rain drops
They wash away
The lady in the
    Maiden landscape

                    Salem 07.27.16

*

Rest on the off season
Routine meal time
    Will remind you
At that absent minded moment
Pounds of pressure
Pounding out the measure
    Of a man
It is a slow birth
The dark night of the soul
Turned to years
Internal turn outward

                Portland, OR 11.22.10

*

Separated we take
Together we make
We are all but
Hypoxic parachuters

Salem 10.26.16

*

Claim to a correlation
Leaving room to disclaim
A line can be drawn
    Between any two points

                    Salem 02.28.14

*

Have a great day
Her words echo in my mind
    Not once, twice- thrice
As I left out in the world
Soon those words I thought
And the voice was my own
I will be under the rubble
    Some other
The day is made

                    Portland, OR 10.25.10

*

Goodness can proceed from evil
    But it does not beget
And all along the way
There is no merit
    In it
For you

                    Portland, OR 07.24.09

*

Bard's anagram
Will take me
Back home

       New Orleans 03.2005

*

Strike-strike, hit twice
    Before you roll the dice
I am in fight shape
Raining strikes
Until the foe has lost fight
Please, please
    Learn to never doubt on me
Down to one knee
We assimilated the same way

        Salem 10.07.15

*

Beats give reference
    To past beats
The drum inside us
The last sonata
Those are the happy songs
In gloom
    The beats dissipate sharply

                Corvallis, OR 10.02.1998

*

Love is youthful
Yet
Youth can be frantic confusion
The soil of many trampled lands
Feel new in tender hands
With love, that soil epiphanic
　　Sprouting seeds

　　　　　Salem 02.20.14

*

Human weakness
    We revere what
    We understand
Power of the lesson
    If we can appreciate
A 360 Degree view, but
From one position

            Salem 04.09.06

*

We climb
And climb and climb and climb
Some more
When at mountains' top
We discover
The oxygen poor air
The jagged cares
The frigid atmos fear
I wont to go

Salem 05.29.16

*

*

*

*

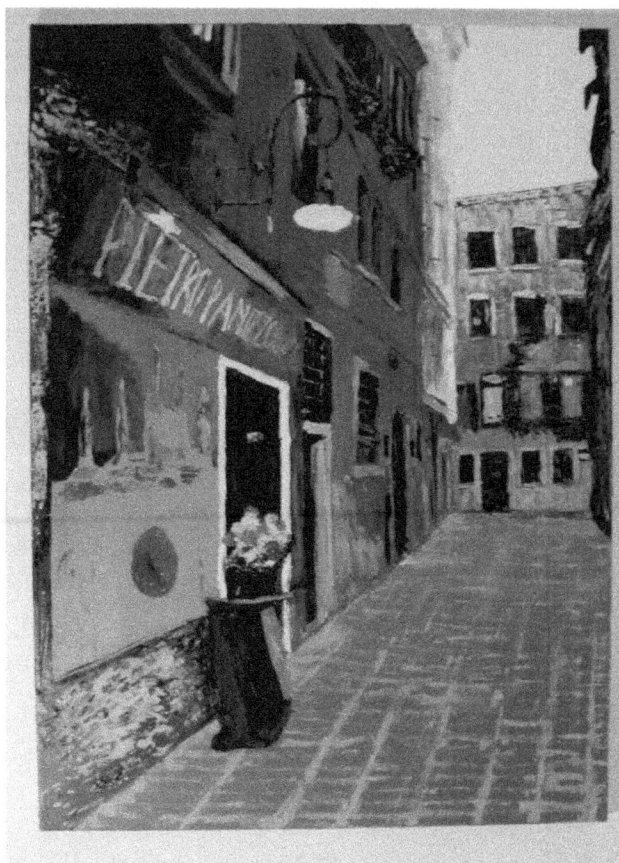

*

*

Brad Dehler's "Cantus" is a litany of meditations that are contextualized by the immense space that can magnify meaning: small phrasings, by design, appear larger on the physical page. This is not incidental. It is the poet's economical task of saying more with less.

Here is a collection that is as philosophical as it is poetic, channeling the existential being-in-thought that breathes life into those unafraid of not knowing. The exhale between "songs" affirms: getting lost in its music is imperfectly okay.

- **Tim'm T. West**, Poet, educator, and author of "Red Dirt Revival", "Flirting", and the latest "pre|dispositions"
TruAtRedDirt@gmail.com

*

*

141

*

www.ingramcontent.com/pod-product-compliance
Lightning Source LLC
Chambersburg PA
CBHW021156020426
42331CB00003B/87